HERO IN YOU

BOUQUET OF POEM

JIGME CHODEN

ISBN 979-888606496-4

For my parents and brothers

And in memory of my late grandmother

Contents

Acknowledgements *vii*

Mend The Broken Ties

Gone From Us

Resolution As The Sunrise

Distant Lovers

You Aren't Afar

You Weren't Mercy

Forgiven, Forgotten, And Forever

Disguised Devil

The SCAR

To The Dripping Moon

Time Really Heals

Am I Late?

Will The Bud Sprout?

Getting On In Years

Rays Of Hope

Salt On Wound

Victory Shall Be Ours

Turn Back The Time

Trouble Pleasure

For How Long?

Freeze Button

Living For Self

Gatekeeper

Contents

To The Dust, He Shall Return

Havoc

Truth Can't Be Swallowed

HERO In You

December Night

Your Arrival

Spring It Is!

The Street Isn't Safe Anymore

Unless A Legend

Folktale And The Village

No Country For Old

Stronger She Has Become

Rise Brothers Rise

Poet In Me

Happiness

Marriage

Stranger

Acknowledgements

I would like to thank everyone who had supported me in every little way in making this a success. I want to thank my siblings for encouraging me to go forward with writing especially poems and my parents for your guidance. I would like to extend my gratitude to the family of Technical Training Institute Rangjung for your support

Mend the broken ties

Days are getting colder,

Tea in my cup is getting warmer.

I see winter conquering its reign,

For Autumn it's surrendered already.

Its arrival will be glamorous.

With frost and dues on the blade of grass.

It neither welcomes you with spring's blossoms

Nor greet like drooping paddy of Autumn;

But with mountains covered with snows.

People locked inside near the fire,

With tea and snacks in front

Yet, a time to mend the broken ties.

Gone from us

Silken knot is slacken

The voice loved is stilled

Cousins met and people gathered

But you went never to return

If only tears could make stairways

Empty hearts could make pathways

I would walk miles to reach your place

Only to bring you back to the family

Those special moments we shared

Are always in my heart

If only I could have you back

I would like to sit with you and talk

Just like we used to do

You are gone from us,

It's the bitter truth we can't hold

Resolution as the sunrise

As New Year made its entrance

Everyone hopes for a better year

Few started to make New Year's resolution

While few plans to celebrate hard

For it is the new beginning

A thousand resolution is made but vary

Habitual drinkers would think of quitting

While smoker promises to stop after that day

Alas! Resolution isn't only for them

Readers think to read more

Writers to write many hymns

Travelers wish to find new excursions with care

Whence it is made

It gives hope and it is a climax

Where a cursed story takes a new route

Like that of a fairy tale

However, few will be done

While rest are left as the sunrise

Distant lovers

May our story be fluttered in the pervading sky

By the winds to the valleys and mountains

That lovers once lived

As in the fairy tale

Longing for them to meet

But the mountains weren't bridged

Yearning to be by the side of each other

But the distance still miles afar

May this story be an inspiration

Especially to the distant lovers

Who finds the reason to love than separate

You aren't afar

The moon shines high up the sky

How I wish to watch its rays with you

To look into your eyes

As it reflects the rays

Mountains, miles, and unending roads

They keep me away from you

But never let my love for you die

Rather the reason to love harder

Though the distance keeps us apart

You aren't away from my heart

I loved you then, now and I will

We shall never be apart

You weren't mercy

You landed your icy Hand

So soon on my lovely friend

He has a lot undone

His only mother, dearest son

Lovely wife and sister

They need him

If only you were mercy

He would've seen his son read

Celebrated the success

He was a lovely friend

He deserves to live some more

Forgiven, forgotten, and forever

It's been such a long time

The pain would still remain

Your decision still would bring me to defeat

All I could wish is to turn back the time

Those past years had been hard

Thoughts of you would cling to me

But I did it all differently

The time heals, it really does

That doomed days wouldn't be erased

Anxious that I wouldn't be giving up easily

It looks so long to completely do away

But time took its pace

Now I remember you

Not with grief

Rather the gratification

That I set you free

I have reached this far

Forgiven, forgotten, and forever

I am no longer a slave to my past

Got this peace of mind in me

Disguised devil

To the devil disguised in god

I worshipped with all my heart

Received pain than blessings

I wish I never worshiped

If it has to be that way in the end

The SCAR

Loving a person like never before

It seems the weakness

One shouldn't possess

Because it is going to leave you a scar

The wound heals faster

But never does the scar

To the dripping moon

Sliver sphere, oh, heavenly eye

The city is asleep but

You are staying up all night

Illuminating with your rays of poem

Untying them from their sorrows and grieves

Your words were their unheard voices

As dawn broke, dews I felt

They weren't dews, you were dripping

Staying up there all by yourself

You were lonely

Time really heals

Days, weeks, and months

Finally, years have passed

As though the world has ended

The first day was tough and hard

Weeks still had the pain lingering in the scars

It seemed more painful than yesterday

Months foresaw no future

Not a silver lingering

The pain of losing you heaped

Of those tougher days

Self-respect is what I realized

Time really heals!

Am I late?

While the flowers turn to fruits

But my tree hasn't got a sprout yet

Am I hate for Autumn?

Will the bud sprout?

The trust, love, and care were all ripped off

Barren, I have become just like the winter trees

They wait for spring hoping for blossoms

And buds to sprout

But my buds of trust, love, and care

Haven't started yet

What will I expect from a skin-dead guitar string and barkless tree?

A little burning hope has no power to become ablaze.

Getting on in years

Winter cold is just around the corner

Autumn bade farewell

It isn't the season that count

But the sign of getting on in years

Clouds leaving the sky clear

Birds returning to their home

Leaves shedding

Leaving the tree barren

Flowers wilting

I see poetry set and ready to leave

Ready to soar up high

As high as the clouds

That no shadow is to be thrown on land

Alas! Define which season I am with

Rays of Hope

The dusk rules out the daylight

Anxiety and uncertainty inducted

However, the dawn breaks through the night

New rays of hope are showered

Borders sealed, Business shut

Schools and institutions closed

Piece by piece we had to adapt

Amid the confusion

Sound of hope came out

The speech of His Majesty

Arose new hope in people

Once again, we are united

Under one leader

With one goal

To fight against the virus

Salt on wound

A lavish businessman hit hard

By the pandemic

He has become passively aggressive

Over the silent social media

Stating bittersweet reasons

To the walking dead

That was false truth never be heard

Catalyst they have become

Salt on bruises

Fuel in fire

All they think is profit

Even when their life is at risk.

Victory shall be ours

From time immemorial

We have been with enemies and wars,

Protecting our land and people.

We celebrated the victory

And it has become our history

Though the future is a mystery

But we promised to let it not be misery

We aren't wary of distancing

If only we can protect our loved ones

We aren't bored of quarantine and lockdown

For we are the responsible citizen

We shall fear not to this virus

For us, we've battled many of its kind then

Now, we shall conquer its reign

VICTORY shall be ours.

Turn back the time

A man was given a job to fix a wall clock

When he was done, he presented

They saw the second-hand tricking anticlockwise

"The clock is moving back," they said in unison

I made it on purpose!

There are people in quarantine and their loved ones at

Home waiting for their arrival

For few, they are at the hand of death and some yet to

Doctors at the frontline risking their life, teachers still educating from home

Business shut down and vehicles don't move

Empty cities

Where distancing from a loved one is considered love

If time is to turn back just like this

Everything will be in reverse

To the aura of love and affection

The time we call "normal"

Trouble pleasure

Empty roads I see through the window

Silence all over, as though the last to survive

People are out only for food

Else they are in like rats

Trouble pleasure it is to stay in

However, a time to mend the broken ties

Over a cup of tea with snacks

Sharing bittersweet memories

In small crowded family memories

For how long?

For how long should I wait to hear from you?

What will I expect from answering breeze?

Like the floating feather, I wander all-day

With you, I expected the life

But in return, you threw ashes

Those words, midnight chats, togetherness

To the dust, they have returned

Still, I yearn for a word to exchange

Freeze button

Characters on the stage like sage

Deeply drowned into their role

When the freeze button is pressed

As though in a freeze-frame

Stiffen they were in their characters

Role of white and orange

Took over the stage

In their monologue said the people are sick

And need to be attended

Living for self

Living for others sounds noble

Many dreams to be humble

But few would conquer

While rest is a distant dream

Not everyone you can please

Only rear few would be

Living for self is the better choice

Contentment should start from within

Then to the rest

Give yourself some time to realize

Then living to the standard others had set

For you aren't programmed, Robert

But a human with a head and heart

Gatekeeper

At the gate, I sat on a chair

Guarding the place

Many passes by with a glance

But not even a smile they wear

Few stops by wanting to enter

But fails to follow protocols

Please sir, could you wear a mask, use the tracing app?

Oh, it is inside my pocket

I forgot my phone

Excuses I shall consider lame

Sorry sir, I can let you in only if you follow those norms

Blushes on their faces and anger in the eyes

We both would be at peace

Only if you follow those norms

To the dust, he shall return

The dawn grew and ripens sun rays

But to evening it shall return

Spring had given birth to blossoms

As though to beautify all days to come

A lotus growing in swampy mud

To the world, they surprised

But it shall return to mud once wilted

As soul without form finally chose one

With loud human cries, it was born

As though to live eons

To the dust, he shall return

Havoc

You reap what you saw

God hasn't applied it really

Maybe she got skipped from the god's list

She worked hard to be successful

Empathy and sympathy are all she wears

Loved them all by heart

Yet she was cheated

She didn't reap she sawed

It aches to have love not reciprocated

For it has no reason to love

It can't be forced either

She decided to stay in lockdown

For she wants to run away

Away from those painful truths

To start all over again

Truth can't be swallowed

She fell to a man at sweet sixteen;

Dropped school after repeating eight for the third time.

Gave birth to her first child at twenty

The husband got promoted to CEO.

Everything happened just so fast.

Soon they had their second child.

Then the family but small was the happiest!

None would expect the fall to them

But God has decided already.

When she would always be nursing her kids' at home

He would leave for office early, reach late at night!

Little ones had no idea of their father having an affair.

She would hear neighbors talking about it in secret

But believed them not unless he was caught red hand

He had decided to leave them blaming on the fate

Their love story was like the downfall of the Roman Empire

All her might built to trust was shattered

She had none but her own self to whom she believed the strength.

Before filing the divorce, he had to rush to the hospital,

For his father was on his death bed. Unfortunately, he breathed his last breath in a car crash.

The kids lost their father to death and grandfather too.

That was totally a tragedy never been featured in films.

HERO in you

Hero in you makes a decent actor on stage,

Though, the Villain role suits you the best.

As you walk on stage like sage,

the audience on the floor is stunned by your talent.

You are the northern star,

Leading crusaders through the way.

The one looked up to for his hidden talents.

Sober you become with challenges;

But with no scar Starts over again.

For you are the man with hopes,

That takes courage to heal with time.

HOWEVER, appearance on with seriousness,

It's the opposite of your loving nature.

While the friendship nourishes,

With those who still want to give.

Adjectives are running brief,

Nothing equals yourself.

For you are the dreamer that bends,

But never to be broken in the end.

Keep burning the hero in you!

December night

That freezing winter night,

Beneath the rays of street lights.

You stood before me and stared,

With your glittering eyes and smiled.

My eyes met yours,

I looked away with a feebly nervy heart.

Wordless we were found,

Though thousands to be told.

Your arrival

As the New Year approach

The human soul Fragile

It presented us with, little baby girl.

She is the first of many.

He declared that they conceived

Later, the doctor told

It will open the door for you.

Excitedly we waited for your arrival.

Your mother knitted tinny socks

Father chose pink

Grandparents were excited

That they will have their blood

Calling them grandparents.

The only niece born.

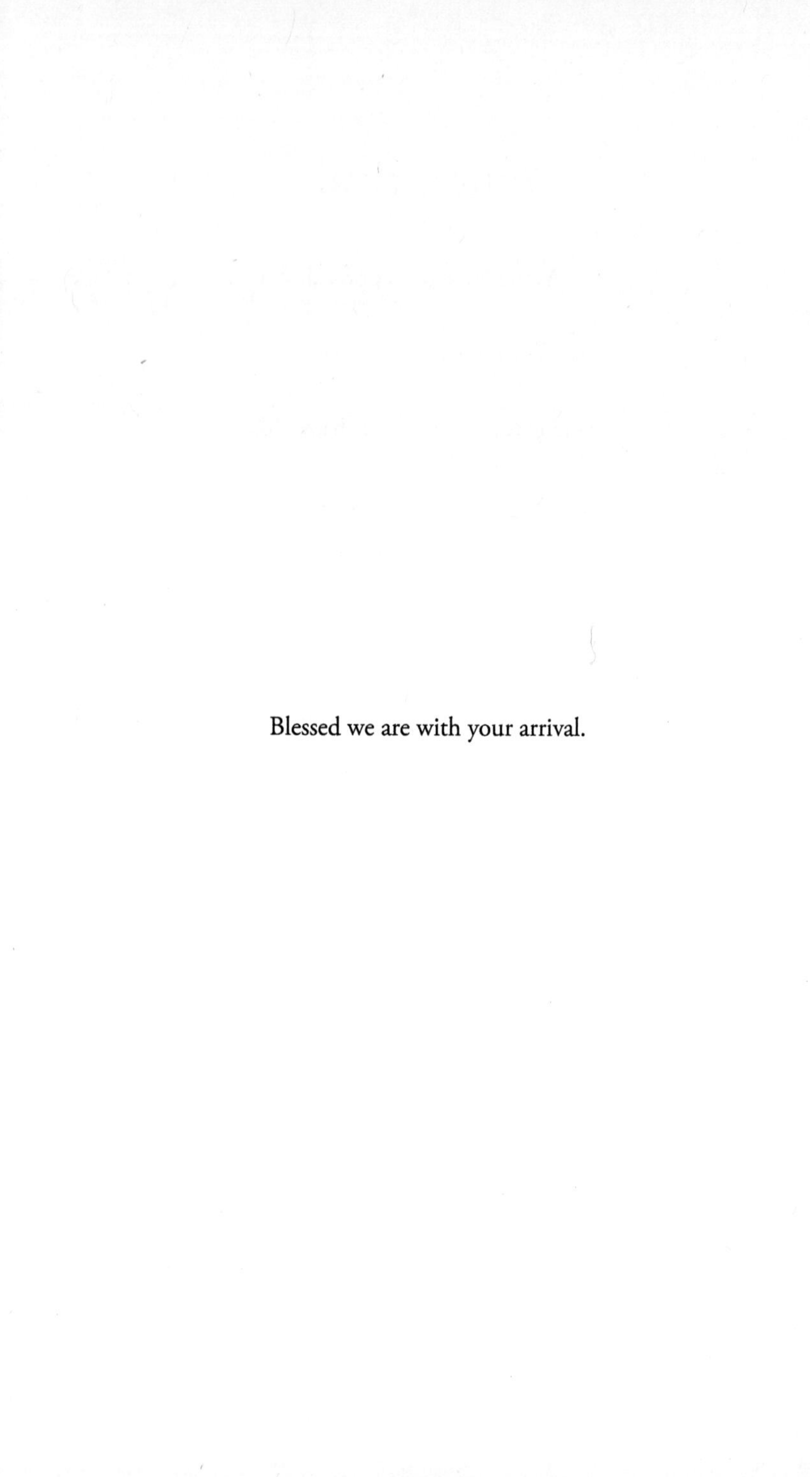

Blessed we are with your arrival.

Spring it is!

Its preceding winter and following summer.

I hear birds chirping in the vernal equinox.

Cuckoo, the harbinger of the message,

Your melodious call makes my sense numb.

Thus, the opening of the cherry marks the start.

Between the two oxen, he stands.

She follows each trail sowing the seeds.

Spring it's associated with renewal and regrowth.

Though it pours,

Farmers stay not at home.

The scorching sun wouldn't tempt them

to rest under the shade.

A roaring sound from above is heard.

Spring it is!

The street isn't safe anymore

Neighbors were their family

Strangers their friends. .

A drunkard would sleep on his way home

Safely he would open eyes at the dawn

Children would play till the sunset

And forget to return home.

Their parents would entrust them to neighbors.

This trend was followed far and wide.

Fear was never for humans then.

Now, children entrusted to Neighbors,

She returns home from school is raped.

A drunkard sleeping on his way home is robbed.

The street once a paradise is unsafe.

Unless a legend

Autumn made its way through.

Golden hues of paddy are born.

Soon their corns will be reaped

And Stored for another season to be sawn.

Death keeps alarming,

Soon its icy hand will be on us

But we think of the better days to come.

Seasons come and go

Trees shed and give bud the next.

Their appearance to an eye is never forgotten

For us, once dead;

We become the story for years

But not for eon

Our names will be erased

Permanently and never to be remembered.

Unless a legend you were.

Folktale and the village

Yakgang, was once a village with yaks.

A man was tempted to own a few

Hidingly took them to his shed.

A Sloppy land, unsuitable for grazing.

Some days later yaks weren't there

But dead they were.Its hair flooded the village

Yakpongang he named the place.

Never did he think that they would die

Had had he known,

would have taken to where they belong.

Before the dawn made his way uphill with a load of meats

Tired he was but never did he give up.

The red flashes were hidden in the bushes,

near the tree

Relieved he was.

The next day went to check on

Adieu! They already bade him farewell

'Shame' he named the place.

Yaks stolen and dead

Their flashes hid and named the villages

Yet a beautiful folktale.

No country for old

That is no country for old men

The young with shiny metal in their hand,

With earphones plugged in the ears.

Head bent to the screen

Scrolls every single page

Sound of the gun as though in the battle field

A patient on the hospital bed

A child crying for attention

An aged man for help

Students with notes piled

But heeded not if the shiny metal is in hand.

Crowded as seas but divided like an enemy

Together but far enough

That is not a country for old men.

Stronger she has become

Death laid its icy hand on her mother

Then a month old calf she was

Her sister lost her only son to the king of death

It was too hard to accept the bitter truth

In their absence

Forlorn and dejected they were

Mother of all gave her a name

'Tshomo' she was named

Now here she is

Her head held high

And fears for nothing

For she already faced the death king

Stronger and bolder she has become.

Rise brothers rise

Rise, rise, brothers rise,

The sun has already shown its rays.

For us left no enough time;

But race uphill with no rest.

Tie your rope around the waist.

Put winter boots and gloves

For ground, the frost has blanketed

as white as snow on the mountain.

Let's race uphill with no rest

And enter the woods with no fear.

Collet dead ones of it kind

For woods, they are our friends.

Poet in me

While yearning for you;

I have seen a hundred sunrise

A thousand dreams of yours.

Had sleepless nights

From dusk to dawn.

While I saw myself drawn into a metaphor,

Unfolding the Petals of the poem.

Unhurriedly playing with words.

Its leaf turned yellow to green,

Poet inside me grew louder.

I would yearn eons o let the poet inside grow louder

And ever louder.

Happiness

In the midst of hustle and bustle,

Forlorn and dejected are the people.

Despite its deepening value,

Forgotten is happiness.

When people care and are connected,

The world become a better place to live in.

Celebrate commonness than what divides,

For life, it's happier when together.

Marriage

Mother looks through the window,

Saw nature hued with meadow

The other side of the mountain

With White Clouds rising like a fountain.

Clearly remembering glimmer days,

Trying hard not to remember though.

Comparing herself to the trees,

Standing up all-weather though tough.

For her marriage was never a choice,

But to serve her parents all through.

An eldest of seven married twice.

Stranger

Better than all beauties

That in flowers are found.

Though appealing and beautiful

It's been blown by the wind

Until it gives out its only scent.

Better than all lights

That in the moon is found

Brightens the dark though

It's been covered by the clouds

Until the dark curtain is drawn

Better than any warmth

That in-person you love is found.

Though cared and loved

They alters with time and distance

Finally become stranger with memories.

Better than any memories

A stranger then friend you've made

Though tries hard to erase them

Are inscribed in blood and bones.

Printed by Libri Plureos GmbH in Hamburg,
Germany